CLIMI
AND WALL PLANTS

ARTHUR HELLYER

HarperCollins*Publishers*

Products mentioned in this book

Benlate* + 'Activex'	contains	benomyl
'Nimrod'-T	contains	bupirimate/pirimicarb
'Roseclear'	contains	bupirimate/pirimicarb /triforine
'Rapid'	contains	pirimicarb
'Sybol'	contains	pirimiphos-methyl

Products marked thus 'Sybol' are trade marks of Imperial Chemical Industries plc
Benlate* is a registered trade mark of Du Pont's
Read the label before you buy: use pesticides safely.

Editors Maggie Daykin, Susanne Mitchell
Designer Chris Walker
Picture research Moira McIlroy

First published 1988 by
HarperCollins Publishers

This edition published 1992

A CIP catalogue record for this book is available from the British Library.

Photoset by Bookworm Typesetting
Printed and bound in Hong Kong by Dai Nippon Printing Company

Front cover: Lonicera periclymenum 'Belgica'
Back cover: Wisteria floribunda macrobotrys
Both photographs by Michael Warren

CONTENTS

INTRODUCTION

Climbers are the 'drapes' of the garden. The functions performed indoors by wallpapers, curtains and coverings are taken over in the open by a great variety of climbing plants and some others that, though not really climbers, can be made to serve a similar purpose by proper pruning and training.

Parthenocissus tricuspidata 'Veitchii', the vigorous and self-clinging vine, seen here in the full glory of its autumnal colouring. The leaves are ovate or trifoliate in form; the fruits dark blue. Provides very dense wall-coverage.

Types of climber True climbers hold themselves aloft by a variety of means. The simplest, seen in climbing roses and the ornamental brambles, is to thrust themselves into shrubs and trees, finding support among the branches and perhaps gaining a little extra hold by means of thorns or prickles. A little more complicated are the twiners, which twist themselves around almost anything that is not too thick. In the wild, like the thrusters, they rely mainly on trees and shrubs for support and by this simple means some – such as the wisterias and climbing honeysuckles – can ascend to considerable heights.

Then there are the tendril climbers, for example, sweet peas, vines and clematis, which modify some of their stems or leaf stalks to coil around anything fairly slender that offers support. In gardens they are happy on trellis, wires or twiggy branches but they cannot cope with a large surface such as a post or thick pillar.

Finally, most ingenious of all, are the self-clingers which even cope with a wall without need for any aids. Some, like the ivies, do it with modified roots which get into the smallest crevices or irregularities and even succeed in holding on to completely smooth surfaces, though not quite so securely. Some of the plants popularly known as Virginia creeper cling with little adhesive pads formed on the ends of tendrils but other Virginia creepers have tendrils without the pads and so need something around which to twist. It is such duplications in the use of popular names that make it essential sometimes to use botanical names – they are more precise. The self-clinging Virginia creeper is *Parthenocissus tricuspidata*, a name that belongs to no other plant.

Some plants treated as climbers have no natural aptitude for climbing; they are really shrubs but with pruning and training can be spread out on walls, along fences or on screens. Many of the shrubs pressed into service as climbers are evergreens, that is, they retain their leaves all winter. Not a great many true climbers do this and are also hardy enough to be grown outdoors in Britain and there are many situations in which it is an advantage to have a covering that remains equally leafy throughout the year.

There are also some true climbers that are herbaceous, that is, they die down in winter and grow up again the following spring. Some twine, some cling by their tendrils and all can be very useful when permanent cover is not required. The most popular fully herbaceous kinds are *Lathyrus grandiflorus*, the Everlasting Pea, *Humulus lupulus* 'Aureus', the Golden Hop and *Tropaeolum speciosum*, the Flame Flower.

Eccremocarpus scaber is a semi-woody climber which out of doors in Britain is usually 'killed' to ground level each winter but in sunny, sheltered places often starts to grow again the following spring so that it really behaves like a herbaceous perennial. According to their local climate, gardeners treat this popular climber as a half-hardy annual, a half-hardy biennial, a herbaceous plant or a shrubby climber. Whatever the system of management, it is always increased by seed.

There are also a number of genuine, annual climbers which can be very useful for quick cover. I have devoted a short section to these (and biennials) as they require special treatment (see pages 14–15).

ABOVE Hederas are good companion plants for vines. Here, the cream and green of *Hedera helix* 'Jubilee' complements the purple foliage of *Vitis vinifera purpurea* and will still clothe the wall when the vine takes its winter rest.

RIGHT Roses and clematis are another popular combination. And both plants will usually oblige with a second flowering if conditions are right.

PLANTING CLIMBERS

Without exception, all of the plants included in this book will grow in any reasonably fertile soil. It does not have to be specially acid or alkaline, it need not be very rich but it does need to be reasonably supplied with plant food. It should also be well dug or forked before the climbers are planted so that the young roots can penetrate it easily. Later on, as they become established, the roots will be able to find their way almost anywhere but at the outset they need assistance.

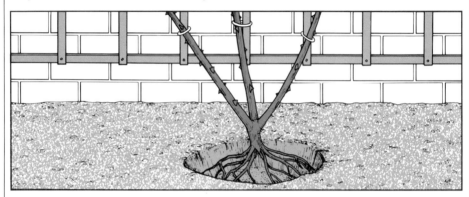

Soil preparation One of the hazards with climbers used to cover walls is that the soil close to a wall is almost always a lot drier than the soil right out in the open. For this reason it is not wise to plant very close to a wall, though this might seem the neatest way of going about it. Some 30–45cm (1–1½ft) away the soil will get more direct rainfall and it will still be possible to bring the stems back to the wall. An area at least 45cm (1½ft) square and as much deep should be prepared for each plant, not just by breaking it up with spade or fork but also by mixing in some manure (it can be the specially prepared bagged type), 'Forest Bark' Ground and Composted Bark, or peat plus a little fertilizer. If the ground is hard or sticky it may be better to remove it altogether from the planting sites and replace with better soil from another part of the garden or from a garden centre.

Roses Climbing plants are almost always supplied by nurserymen well established in containers from which they can be transplanted at any time of the year. An exception may be climbing roses, especially if purchased from a rose specialist. Then delivery is likely to be in the autumn or winter and the plants will have been lifted from the open ground. There will be no soil on the roots, so they must either be re-planted immediately where they are to grow or have their roots well covered with soil to keep them moist until it is convenient to plant them permanently.

There is nothing wrong with bare root planting provided it is done well and promptly while the plants are leafless. Advantages are that the plants will probably have a more outward searching root system and that a greater selection of varieties may be available.

Other plants In general, plants lifted from the open ground will require wider planting holes than those removed from containers since the roots of the former should be spread out in a natural way. When planting in autumn and winter it may be wise also to loosen the outer roots of container plants and lead them out into the surrounding soil but it is unwise to cause root disturbance when planting in summer.

With all planting the aim should be to cover the uppermost roots with from 2.5–5cm (1–2in) of soil. Deep planting will retard growth; shallow planting may allow some roots to dry out and be killed. With container plants, a safe rule is to cover the ball of soil with 2.5cm (1in) of the new soil. With bare root plants the old soil mark can usually be seen on the stems and this should also be buried to a depth of 2.5cm (1in).

Unless the soil is very wet, water after planting giving at least a gallon per plant to settle the soil in around the roots. When planting in spring or summer, frequent repeat waterings are likely to be necessary until the plants are growing strongly. Give the water direct from an open hose (but with slow water flow to prevent soil being washed off the roots) or from the spout of a watering can and be sure to give enough to soak well into the soil. If the ground has been properly prepared no feeding will be required for the first two or three months and after that it will depend on the time of year and the degree of growth being made (see page 19).

Growing in containers Climbing plants of all kinds can also be grown permanently in large containers. Tubs or planters holding 100 litres (22 gal) of soil are about the minimum for permanent climbers of any kind. It is better to use a soil-based, rather than a peat-based compost because of its longer life and greater capacity to hold a good reserve of plant food. If garden soil is used, at least one third its own bulk of peat should be mixed with it to ensure good aeration combined with reasonable moisture holding; also add a slow release compound fertilizer such as John Innes base at the rate advised by the manufacturer.

OPPOSITE, ABOVE Always plant climbers at least 30–45cm (1–1½ft) from a wall to avoid problems of dryness.

RIGHT Some climbers can also be trailers, and make excellent ground cover. Here, *Hedera colchica variegata* outlines a pathway while, in the container, another hedera begins to climb the new brick wall. Quite a number of climbers can be container grown.

HOW TO USE CLIMBERS

Climbers can be used to clothe walls or fences, or be allowed to cover arches and pergolas, or be trained up posts, pillars and tripods and over arbours and screens of many kinds or they may simply be permitted to find their own natural way among the branches of trees and shrubs. Sometimes one sturdy type of climber can be used to support a more fragile-stemmed climber, such as a clematis or a sweet pea, and these combinations can produce delightful effects. The use that is to be made of the plants will have a bearing both on their selection and on the way in which they are grown.

The prolifically flowering *Hydrangea petiolaris* (climbing hydrangea) provides attractive screening for a less than perfect wall or, as here, a tree stump. However, this vigorous self-clinger will require judicious cutting back from time to time where space is restricted.

Trees or shrubs used as supports for climbers. In such instances, it should not be overlooked that the hosts may be retarded by their companions. Ivy will ascend to the top of high trees and, though it does little harm in the early years, once it erupts from the top and commences to form a canopy it can soon kill the tree. The Russian Vine, *Polygonum baldschuanicum*, can also grow right over the top of trees and some very vigorous wild roses will do the same. They can look spectacular when their flowers cascade from a great height but it would be unwise to subject one's best trees to this kind of competition. Sometimes old orchard trees, no longer of much use for cropping, are worth retaining as living supports for the more moderately vigorous climbing or rambler roses and clematis. Many of the summer flowering varieties of clematis can be cut hard back each year, in late winter or early spring, and this restricts their growth sufficiently to make them very acceptable companions even for some medium size shrubs or they can be allowed to thread their way over a close carpet of heather. However, all such schemes require close attention to ensure that they do not get out of hand and a readiness to prune if there is any risk to the host plant.

Walls and fences can provide all the support necessary for self-clinging climbers such as ivies, ampelopsis and the climbing hydrangeas, *Hydrangea petiolaris, Schizophragma integrifolium, S. hydrangioides* and *Pileostegia viburnoides*, but with all these there is a danger that growth will extend too far and penetrate beneath tiles or block up gutters and waterpipes. The popular belief that such plants harm bricks, stones or concrete is false but they may hasten the decay of woodwork and, unless kept in check, can make painting and other maintenance work more difficult. Against this must be weighed the advantage that the plants will require no extra support, no nails, vine eyes or trellis, and that they will need virtually no maintenance except for occasional pruning simply to keep them within reasonable bounds.

ABOVE Semi- or full shade is best for *Lonicera tellmanniana,* a hybrid with orange-yellow, terminal clusters of flowers in mid-summer. A strong-growing, deciduous climber here lending its brightness to a pillar well suited to the plant's twining habit.

LEFT The evergreen Pyracanthas can be pruned to suit the requirements of their 'host'. This particularly well-trained *Pyracantha* 'Orange Glow' hugs the house wall without the sacrifice of berries that such pruning can demand.

Ugly walls can be made beautiful with climbers and those that are in poor condition may actually be preserved by the protection the foliage gives from frost, damp and atmospheric pollution.

Twiners and tendril climbers on walls will need some additional support. It can be wires strained between vine eyes driven into the masonry, trellis fixed in any convenient way but not pressed so tightly against the wall that stems or tendrils cannot get around it, or netting either of coated or galvanized wire or of nylon. Each has its merits and drawbacks but probably horizontal wires strained 2.5cm (1in) out from the wall and at about 30 cm (1ft) vertical spacing is as neat and convenient as anything.

To avoid making too many holes in a wall, it may be desirable to attach a wooden framework firmly to it and then fix the wires to the wood. What must always be borne in mind is that the weight of a vigorous climber is considerable and so the support, whatever its nature, must be firmly secured or in time it will inevitably collapse.

Other supports For the above reason flimsily built arches are also a menace. They need to be strong and firmly anchored in the soil. Pergolas must be sturdily constructed with substantial uprights and roof members. If wires are strained along each side of a pergola, climbers can be trained along them and the whole thing converted into a plant tunnel. Alternatively, plants can be confined to the pillars and the roof members, the interspaces between the uprights being left open to the air, rather in the manner of a cloister.

A mellow brick wall is an asset to be highlighted rather than concealed. And what could be more complementary than *Chaenomeles speciosa*, with clusters of fiery red flowers in early spring and greenish-yellow edible fruits in autumn. When it is wall-trained, this climber should be pruned after its flowering.

Climbers grown on single vertical poles can be convenient since they occupy little lateral space but the poles need to be deeply sunk in the soil if they are to remain upright for long when burdened with growth. It is easier to obtain stability with tripods lashed or nailed together at the top but, inevitably, these occupy a good deal more ground.

A considerable variety of arbours can be purchased and all can be used as supports for climbers if so desired. Metal arbours are more likely to survive for a long time than wooden ones and tendril climbers will find the relatively slim metal bars congenial for support. All wood used for supporting plants should be rot proof either by its own nature, for example, western red cedar or an African hardwood, or through impregnation with a rot repellant. Creosote is best avoided as in hot weather it can give off fumes that scorch plants. However, this danger is much greater under glass than outdoors.

Whole patios or courtyards, or sections of them, can be covered with climbers to make pleasant outdoor rooms. The roof can be formed of rafters in a similar manner to a pergola or with strained wire but even stout wire is apt to sag in time if the spans are greater than 1.2m (4ft). Much depends on the type of climber chosen and the degree of pruning it receives. Vines heavily pruned both in winter and summer make a fairly light yet attractive canopy for a sitting-out area.

ABOVE A really well-constructed pergola provides an ideal framework for the more rampant climbers. *Rosa* 'Seagull' with its lovely, massed flowers is one such grateful tenant.

LEFT Another popular climbing rose, 'American Pillar' clambers up its sturdy support, forming an archway of deep pink flowerheads.

13

Annual climbers One should not overlook the possibility of supplementing perennial climbers by introducing annual or biennial kinds. These must be renewed annually from seed but this is cheap to buy and mostly easy to germinate. There is no difficulty in growing sweet peas, either by sowing them in a greenhouse, frame or sunny window in early spring or outdoors, where they are to grow, in April–May. There are now varieties of many different heights, some so short that they scarcely seem to be climbers, others, such as the Jet Set and Galaxy types range from 90cm–2.1m (3–7ft) and are neither so dense nor so heavy in growth that they will harm anything.

The same cannot be claimed for climbing nasturtiums which make a lot of growth and have quite big leaves that exclude a lot of light. But they grow at express speed, their scarlet, orange and yellow colours are very bright and seed can be sown outdoors from mid-April to mid-May where the plants are to bloom. Nasturtiums are ideal to make a dense screen or cover for unsightly objects.

Another very fast growing climber to raise from seed is *Cobaea scandens*. It is really a perennial but seldom survives the winter outdoors in Britain and grows so rapidly from seed that it is usually treated as a half-hardy annual. This means sowing in a warm greenhouse in February-March, potting the seedlings individually and acclimatizing them so that they can be planted outdoors safely in late May or early June. The flowers are rather like those of Canterbury Bells – in fact the popular name is Cathedral Bells – and they are either purple or greenish-white. There are seldom enough of them to be spectacular but they look very pretty peeping out among other things. *Eccremocarpus scaber*, popularly known as the Glory Flower, though strictly a soft-stemmed perennial, is also often grown as a half-hardy annual in the same way as a cobaea. It has much divided ferny leaves and slender stems provided with tendrils and abundant little tubular flowers in orange, yellow or red, all summer.

The Morning Glories, of which the best are *Ipomaea* 'Heavenly Blue', wholly blue, and *I.* 'Flying Saucers', blue and white, are very spectacular when doing well but they need warmth and sunshine to bring out their best. They are genuine half-hardy annuals, needing the same treatment as cobaea but with more warmth, around 24°C, 75°F for germination. Young plants of both cobaea and ipomaea can be purchased in most garden centres in May-June. Unfortunately, eccremocarpus is seldom on offer.

Yet another useful, fast-growing climber is the annual hop, *Humulus japonicus*, which can reach 4.5m (15ft) in a few months. It has little beauty of flower but the leaves are handsome and there is a white variegated variety. It is hardy and so can be sown outdoors, in a sunny position. In fact, once established it is likely to produce many self-sown seedlings which may become a nuisance. Do not confuse this plant with the perennial hop which will live for years and has a beautiful golden leaved variety.

OPPOSITE, FAR LEFT *Cotoneaster horizontalis* vies for attention with the equally bright *Jasminum nudiflorum*; a stunning combination. But the Jasmine needs firm control.

OPPOSITE, NEAR LEFT The rather tender *Fremontia californica*, teamed here with *Euryops pectinata* and *Rosa anemoides*.

ABOVE *Ipomaea purpurea* can be spectacular when given the right conditions.

RIGHT Fast-growing *Humulus japonica* 'Aureus' taking a pergola in its stride.

Regular care Climbing and rambler roses (the main difference between them is that the ramblers are laxer in growth and make more of their new stems from the base) are trained against walls, on fences or on poles, pillars, tripods, arches and pergolas. In all these places their stems must be tied in regularly or they will flop all over the place. The only way in which they can become self-supporting, or largely so, is when planted beside trees or shrubs into which they can scramble. Some ramblers, of which 'Max Graff' is a well known example, are sometimes grown as ground cover with no support of any kind or are allowed to tumble down steep banks.

What has been said of the climbing roses is also true of all the other thrusters or scramblers which, in the wild, either sprawl or find support among other stiffer stemmed plants. If this is not a convenient way to grow them in the garden their stems must be tied regularly to any of the supports suggested for roses. Tying in is a time consuming task and, with roses and the ornamental brambles, often a prickly one, though there are thornless or nearly thornless varieties. It is particularly necessary to keep all these plants under control if they are grown on house walls or used to cover arches and pergolas.

Flowers and foliage When choosing climbing plants, most people will think of their flowers first. Yet flowers rarely last for long. The wonderful display of wisteria, for example, is over in a couple of weeks and the highly popular *Clematis montana* only retains its flowers for about a week longer. Most of the garden varieties of clematis have a much longer season though it can be patchy just as the so-called repeat flowering roses concentrate most of their display in a few summer weeks with much smaller but very welcome quantities of bloom later.

By contrast, foliage is there for much longer, all the year if it is evergreen and for at least six months if it is deciduous. The leaves of vines and of the related ampelopsis are beautiful in shape and some kinds colour richly before they fall in the autumn. Actinidias are grown solely for their leaves and so, of course, are ivies except when they start to flower and fruit and then they turn bushy and cease to climb. It is wise to consider this carefully when choosing climbers for the garden and include a fair proportion that have good foliage.

Fruits Also one should think of fruits and ripening seeds for autumn effect. Most spectacular are the scarlet- and orange-berried Firethorns (pyracantha) which are shrubs, not climbers, but readily trained against walls. *Cotoneaster horizontalis* is also a shrub which spreads horizontally in the open but will flatten itself like a fan against a wall when it serves the same purpose as a climber and needs no support. It has neat little leaves which turn coppery red before they fall in the autumn, at which season it is also covered with bright red berries.

Celastrus orbiculatus is grown for its scarlet seeds, displayed against yellow seed capsules, and some clematis cover their seeds with beautiful silken filaments which aid their widespread distribution by wind.

FAR LEFT *Rosa* 'Golden Showers', a beauty well worth regular care.

LEFT *Clematis montana* 'Tetra Rose' tends to grow tall before branching out.

ABOVE Undemanding *Cotoneaster horizontalis* makes a colourful hedge or self-supporting wall plant.

RIGHT Delicate but lovely and prolific, Lathyrus, here cordon grown.

AFTERCARE AND PRUNING

The two things most likely to prevent climbers from getting a good start are dryness and wind. Walls, fences and even pergolas are likely to deflect some rain, so making the soil close to them drier than it would otherwise be. Walls and fences can also cause strong draughts and unexpected turbulence. So in the early stages it may be necessary to water freely and frequently and it may also be desirable to shelter the young growth a little with fine mesh nylon netting or anything similar that will break the force of the wind without stifling the plants.

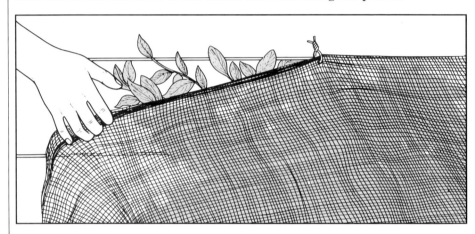

Winter protection Later on, as roots spread out widely, climbers will be able to look after themselves most of the time but there may be some rather tender kinds, such as the Passion Flower *(Passiflora caerulea)*, the Potato Vines *(Solanum crispum* and *S. jasminoides)* and the Trumpet Vines *(Tecoma radicans* and *T. Mdme. Galen)* which, in all but the mildest parts of Britain, will benefit from some protection every winter. One of the advantages of growing plants against walls is the ease with which they can be protected by draping fine-mesh netting over them. Also, remain watchful for severe dryness near walls and beneath trees. It is sometimes necessary to leave a hose or a sprinkler running for a while to restore good growing conditions.

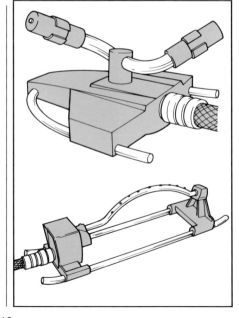

Feeding It is easy to forget this and equally easy to forget that climbers, just like other plants, need food. There are some vigorous kinds, such as wisterias and Russian Vine *(Polygonum baldschuanicum)*, that will scarcely ever need any extra encouragement but at the other extreme the very large-flowered varieties of clematis can do with a lot of help. For success they rely on strong new growth each spring and summer and without feeding they are unlikely to make it.

The same is true of climbing and rambler roses though the real monsters, like Kiftsgate, *Rosa multiflora, R. filipes* and *R. longicuspis*, belong to the self-help league.

Both organics and inorganics have a part to play. The really bulky organics, such as farmyard manure, stable manure, garden compost and old mushroom compost, used as thick top dressings, are most useful if spread while the soil is still moist from winter rain. Inorganic fertilizers as liquid or granules are applied occasionally as a light dressing between April and August.

There is seldom any need to use anything out of the ordinary. A well balanced nitrogen, phosphorus and potash fertilizer such as ICI Liquid Growmore or ordinary granular Growmore will meet most requirements. The liquid is diluted as advised and applied from a can; the granules are lightly peppered over the surface for about 90cm (3ft) around the base of each plant, a first application in April with more to follow in early June and late July when demand will be at its height.

OPPOSITE, TOP Protect newly-planted climbers with a mesh screen, supported by canes, to deter cats and foil frosts.

LEFT A sprinkler soon repays the investment.

RIGHT Slow to establish itself but then a true climber, *Rosa* 'Kiftsgate' – here trained on a frame – would just as happily climb a tree unaided. But make sure that the tree is up to the challenge; those enormous trusses of flowers are very heavy!

Tying is only essential for those plants that do not twist or cling of their own accord. Roses are by far the most numerous and important and, if not carefully and regularly tied in they can become a nuisance. Since there is a constant renewal of growth with these, as with the ornamental brambles, string is as good a material as any for tying. It does not last very long but it does not need to do so and has the great advantage of being very easy to cut and remove.

A difficulty with roses is that, though it is easiest to tie with bare fingers, these are terribly exposed to sharp thorns. It is much easier with two people, one wearing thorn-proof gloves and holding the stems in position, while the other ties them in barehanded. The best compromise, if no helper is available, is to wear tough but flexible gloves which may not give full protection but make'it possible to tie a knot. Some may prefer to use flexible wire which can be twisted with one hand. There are also numerous proprietary ties, some very effective but most rather expensive if you need several.

Pruning The most important maintenance task with climbers is pruning. It is almost impossible to grow roses satisfactorily without it and bad pruning can ruin the result. The quality of bloom of garden varieties of clematis can be improved by pruning and the performance of wistarias is also considerably influenced. Vines must be pruned to prevent them becoming a dense tangle of growth and ivies must be prevented from suffocating other plants. Most of this work is much easier than some of the experts make it appear.

ROSES Though stems will survive for many years, getting thicker and harder in the process, it is the young growth, much of it no more than one year old, that produces most of the good flowers. So each winter one tries to cut out as many of the older stems as possible without losing too much young growth.

With vigorous ramblers such as 'American Pillar' and 'Dorothy Perkins' this is easy since they make a lot of long, young stems from near the base. During the summer these

LEFT A wooden trellis, securely fixed to the wall by means of battens, allows air to circulate behind the foliage. Essential for climbers without their own support system, such as the semi-hardy *Abutilon vitifolium* 'Veronica Tennant'.

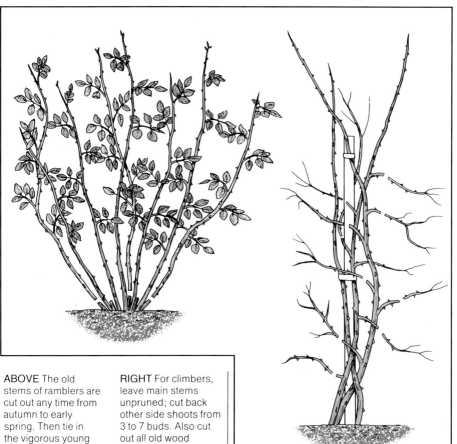

ABOVE The old stems of ramblers are cut out any time from autumn to early spring. Then tie in the vigorous young ones to replace them.

RIGHT For climbers, leave main stems unpruned; cut back other side shoots from 3 to 7 buds. Also cut out all old wood where possible.

can be tied to one side away from the flowering stems and then, when all the flowers have faded or at any time after that until the following March, the old stems can be cut out and the vigorous young ones tied in to take their place.

Many climbing roses, especially those that flower most of the summer, do not make such a clear distinction between old and new growth. Some of the good new stems may come from the base but many branch out from old stems, higher up, and so one must compromise. The aim is still to cut out as much as possible of the old wood but some of

this can only be cut back as far as the good new growth coming from it. One must study the space available and go on cutting out and tying in until it is comfortably filled with healthy young growth. What remains can then be removed.

The ornamental brambles more or less settle the matter for themselves since they allow their old stems to die when they have finished their year; it is then quite clear that they need to be cut out. Some of the weaker young stems can be removed with them if there are too many developing stems left for the amount of space that is available.

CLEMATIS thrive on young growth on which all the flowers are carried. Those that do not start to flower until mid-June or later can, if desired, be cut hard back each February-March, even to within 30cm (1ft) of ground level. This will reduce the size of the plant but may also increase the size of the flowers. Even in February, growth is usually starting so it is easy to see where one can make a pruning cut and be sure of getting a new shoot. This early pruning is not feasible with spring and early summer flowering kinds which have by then made the growth from which they will flower but they can be considerably thinned or cut back immediately after flowering if they threaten to occupy too much space.

HONEYSUCKLES All the popular honeysuckles produce their flowers in a slightly different way, carried on short new growth which comes direct from much longer stems made the previous year. Often they can be left to fend for themselves with little or no pruning but if they start to lose vigour this can be restored by cutting out some of the older growth immediately the flowers fade and supplementing this by feeding and watering. Where space is restricted, honeysuckles can be pruned annually after flowering but with care to preserve plenty of the new growth which will be in evidence by then.

ABOVE
Honeysuckles are fairly self-sufficient, space-invaders; if pruning becomes necessary, take care to preserve the new growth.

RIGHT Two *Clematis* × *Jackmanii* frame a window with their huge, deep violet flower heads. *C. viticella* (far right) should be hard pruned in February or March.

WISTERIAS AND VINES flower on young side growths and plants can be allowed to make a permanent framework of old stems that will get increasingly thick and woody with age. From this side growths are allowed to form but in summer each is shortened to about 15cm (6in). For extra neatness, these pruned shoots can be further shortened to about 2.5cm (1in) in winter. By these means these normally rather rampant climbers can be restricted to quite small areas.

SHRUBS that are trained against walls or fences must be pruned to alter their shape from all-round branching to growth virtually in one plane only. Most of this can be done in summer, after the plants have flowered. Then any good stems for which there is space, and which are sufficiently well placed or flexible to be tied in, are retained.

Other stems for which there is no room or which grow too stiffly away from wall or fence are either cut right out or are shortened to a few centimetres/inches. This is particularly useful with ceanothus, chaenomeles and pyracantha, all of which make flower buds freely on such shortened stems. By contrast, *Forsythia suspensa* and chimonanthus flower better on long stems and so it will be helpful to get as much as possible of this tied in at full length. When pruning fruit-bearing shrubs, retain as much as possible of the fruit and by June–July it will be possible to see where this is.

General care Many climbers can be left unpruned for years but always remove dead or damaged growth as soon as it is noted. If a plant grows too far it can be thinned or cut back as necessary, the best time for this being February–March unless the

TOP Vines need careful, systematic pruning if they are to give of their best.

ABOVE *Forsythia suspensa* and *Clematis alpina*. The former needs tieing in.

plant flowers in spring or early summer when it is better to leave pruning until after flowering. Ivies can be cut back at any time and, when grown on walls, can be freshened up in May–June by clipping them with shears or hedge trimmers. Then the plant can be well brushed to rid it of accumulated debris, which can be considerable.

PROPAGATION

Because of their long, flexible stems it is often quite easy to increase climbing plants by layering. Some will even do it for themselves, making roots from stems which remain in contact with the soil for a considerable time. Quite apart from this obliging – and occasionally irritating – self-sufficiency, climbers can quickly and economically be propagated from cuttings. If you have patience, and in some cases perseverance, they can also be successfully raised from seed.

The best time for layering a clematis is May to June. Gently bend the selected stem and peg down as described in the text (below left). Leave until the following March before detaching from the parent and transplanting.

Layering While climbers will often root from stems of their own accord, the process can be made more reliable by selecting stems one or two years old, making a small wound in each at a joint that can be brought down to the soil and then burying this 2.5cm (1in) or so deep and holding it firmly in place with a stone or peg. A joint is the point at which a leaf is, or was, attached to a stem and it is from this that roots are most readily formed. A wound restricts the flow of sap and promotes root formation. The most efficient methods of wounding for this purpose are either to make a slit through the joint or to draw a knife round the stem just below the joint, cutting sufficiently deep to penetrate the skin without severing the stem. Root formation can be hastened by dusting the wound with hormone rooting powder or dabbing it with a rooting solution or gel.

Layers can be made at any time of year but late spring/early summer is usually a favourable time. When the layer has made some good roots, which is unlikely to be in less than a year, it can be severed from its parent, lifted carefully with as much soil as possible still around them and replanted elsewhere.

Cuttings can be quicker than layers and require much less material. They should be prepared from 12–15cm (4–6in) long pieces of firm current year's growth (it is usually necessary to wait until July for this) and should be severed immediately below a joint. The lower leaves are then removed, the base of the cutting is dipped in rooting powder, liquid or gel and inserted in a half and half mixture of peat and either perlite or gritty sand in a small flower pot. This should then be placed in a propagator or in a polythene bag sealed to retain moist air inside. The cuttings, whether in a propagator or bags, should have plenty of light but it is best not to expose them to strong direct sunlight which may scorch them. As soon as roots begin to form, growth will resume; a few weeks later the cuttings can be potted individually in a peat or soil-based potting compost and grown on until large enough to be planted out where they are to grow. There are advantages in keeping them in a frame until they are sturdy enough to thrive outside.

Seed Some climbers can also be raised from seed which is usually best sown as soon as ripe but if this is impossible, sow the following spring. It is best to sow in pans or seed trays and any standard peat or soil-based seed compost can be used. The seeds can be germinated out of doors or in a greenhouse or frame. Germination of some species can be slow and erratic so do not throw away seed containers for at least eighteen months, and keep looking.

ABOVE Hederas will happily propagate themselves – rooting wherever a trailing stem touches soil. But if you want to speed up the process, any number of stem cuttings can be taken and then planted six to a pot.

LEFT Sowing seeds of climbers in peat pots means that you can plant them out without root disturbance, later.

PESTS AND DISEASES

Climbers suffer from many of the pests and diseases that afflict other plants but, with the exception of some varieties of rose, are not often severely affected. Mildews, rusts and leaf spots of various kinds may infect them and greenfly, blackfly and other aphids may suck the sap from their young shoots and leaves.

No one chemical will deal with all of these but some manufacturers prepare mixtures of pesticides with a wide spectrum of efficacy. An excellent example is 'Roseclear', manufactured by ICI which, as its name implies, has been prepared primarily for roses but can be used safely and effectively on all ornamental climbing plants. It provides a simple method of dealing with all greenfly or blackfly or fungal diseases likely to be encountered. Alternatively, to control other pests, 'Sybol' can be used alone or in a mixture with 'Nimrod'–T or Benlate + 'Activex' for combined pest and disease control. If desired, the two can be mixed in the same sprayer.

If such all-embracing remedies are applied at least three times a year, first in May, again in June and a third time in late July or early August, there should not be much to worry about. But here are a few more specific recommendations regarding the more common pests and diseases for those who prefer not to use blanket treatments.

Aphids The name covers greenfly and blackfly which are slow moving and likely to be found mainly on the new growth. Aphids can multiply at a prodigious rate when conditions are favourable, particularly from May-September. Pirimicarb, marketed as 'Rapid', can kill them within 30 minutes and does not affect other insects, including the industrious bees and ladybirds.

Aphids on rose bud.

Red Spider Mites These are so small that a lens may be required to identify them. They live mainly on the undersides of leaves, particularly along the veins, and they thrive in hot, dry weather when there may be so many of them sucking sap that leaves become mottled with grey or yellow. Many of the insecticides in common use do not kill these tiny mites but pirimiphos-methyl, available as 'Sybol', will. Thorough spraying or hosing with water will also reduce numbers of mites greatly as they hate dampness.

'Sybol' can also be used to control other garden pests if they look like becoming a problem.

Mildew Leaves and sometimes stems become covered with white or grey powdery mould. This is common on roses, especially when the air is damp and the soil dry, and may also be troublesome on vines. Spraying with 'Nimrod'-T or Benlate + 'Activex' will control it.

Rust Another fairly common rose disease. The undersides of leaves are covered with little orange spots and the leaves turn yellow and drop. Spraying with 'Nimrod'-T as soon as rust is noticed gives control.

Advanced stage of mildew.

Black Spot Specific to roses and common on some varieties. Black spots appear on the leaves and rapidly extend to cover and destroy them. Spraying with 'Nimrod'-T or Benlate + 'Activex' will give control but it is wise to alternate these fungicides to prevent the emergence of resistant strains of the fungus.

Weevils Most likely to be troublesome on vines. Black beetle-like insects eat holes in the leaves and larvae feed on the roots. Either spray the foliage or drench the soil with 'Sybol'.

Clematis Wilt Leaves and young stems suddenly collapse. Once every fortnight in April and May spray with Benlate + 'Activex' or a copper fungicide such as Bordeaux Mixture.

Leaf-rolling Sawfly Sometimes widespread on roses. Leaves roll up lengthwise due to attack by small grubs. As a preventive, spray the foliage with 'Sybol'.

Black Spot, specific to roses.

Leaf-rolling Sawfly.

CHOICE CLIMBERS

Whether you want to provide privacy in a town garden, lend fragrance to a patio, draw attention to a mellow brick wall, graceful arbour or stylish pergola – or simply perhaps to blot out a sore on the landscape that cannot be literally removed – there's more than one willing and able climber to meet your needs. Here is a selection of the choicest, each with its special attributes, all sure to give lasting pleasure and widely available at garden centres.

Abutilon megapotamicum

Deciduous shrub. A slender stem-med plant that will sprawl unless tied to a support. It is excellent for a sunny wall against which it can grow 1.8m (6ft) high and produce an abundance of little yellow and red lantern shaped flowers all summer. It will survive a little frost but may be cut to ground level or even killed in severe winters.

Abutilon vitifolium

Deciduous shrub. A tall, rather sparsely branched shrub that can be trained against a sunny wall. The leaves are vine-shaped and covered with down, the mallow-type flowers are soft violet or white and come in June–July. It is fairly hardy but not usually long lived, though readily renewable either from seed or from summer cuttings.

Actinidia chinensis

Deciduous twiner. Popularly known as Chinese Gooseberry because of its edible fruits but these are only pro-duced by female plants in the pre-sence of a male. It is most valuable for its large rounded leaves and stems covered in red hairs when young. It can easily reach 9m (30ft) and is useful for quick coverage of unsightly objects and to give a sub-tropical effect. Will grow in full sun or light shade.

Actinidia kolomikta

Deciduous twiner. A much more slender stemmed plant than the last, grown for its leaves which are heavi-ly splashed with pink and cream when young. It is at its best in May–June. It will reach 3m (10ft), likes sun and warmth and is fairly hardy but young leaves and shoots may be damaged by frost in spring.

Azara microphylla

Evergreen shrub. A slenderly bran-ched shrub with small, dark green leaves and little tufts of yellow, very sweetly scented flowers in winter and early spring. There is a variety with cream variegated leaves. It is a little tender and so best trained against a south- or west-facing wall.

Distinctive mallow-type flowers of *Abutilon megapotamicum*.

Actinidia kolomikta

Camellia reticulata
Evergreen shrub. The long stems lend themselves to training against a wall and this is often the best place for this handsome camellia which is just a little tender. 'Captain Rawes', with very large, semi-double carmine flowers in March-April, is a fine form.

Ceanothus impressus
Evergreen shrub. In the open this makes a densely branched bush but with careful pruning and tying it can be trained against a wall. It is one of the hardiest and most beautiful of the Californian Lilacs which produces abundant thimble-shaped clusters of small, scented, deep blue flowers in April–May. 'Puget Blue' is a good form and very popular. Plant in a sunny position.

Ceanothus thyrsiflorus
Evergreen shrub. A much taller, less widely branched shrub than the last, and therefore easier to train against a wall, but the blue flowers are not quite such a fine colour. It can reach a height of 6m (20ft). A variety named 'Cascade' has larger flower clusters and arching stems which must be allowed some freedom.

Ceanothus veitchianus
Evergreen shrub. Much like the last but the leaves are a brighter green and the flowers a deeper blue. It is not likely to grow quite so tall.

Celastrus orbiculatus
Deciduous twiner. A very vigorous plant excellent for quick coverage of unsightly buildings. It is grown for its seed pods which are unremarkable until they split open to reveal scarlet seeds on a yellow interior. It is essential to obtain the hermaphrodite form which bears both male and female flowers or there will be no seeds. This form must be increased by layers or cuttings since seedlings may be of one sex only.

Ceanothus thyrsiflorus

31

Chaenomeles speciosa 'Moerloosii'

Chaenomeles speciosa
Deciduous shrub. This is the shrub many people know as 'Japonica'. It is a Japanese quince which produces its bright red flowers from December until April and follows them with large, scented fruits. There are numerous colour variations such as 'Nivalis', white; 'Moerloosii', also called 'Apple Blossom', pink and white and 'Rubra Grandiflora', crimson. All will grow and flower in full sun or semi-shade. Considerable pruning is required to deal with their abundant growth.

Chimonanthus praecox
Deciduous shrub. This is the Winter Sweet, so called because of the very sweet perfume of its not very conspicuous greenish-yellow and purple flowers from January to March. It benefits from the protection of a sunny wall against which it is easy to train its long stems.

Chimonanthus fragrans

Clematis 'Hagley Hybrid'

Clematis alpina

Deciduous, tendril climber. This is very different from the popular image of a clematis. The flowers are small, skirt-shaped and nodding, blue or light pink with a tuft of white in the centre; they come in April–May. 'Francis Revis' is a good blue and white variety. All forms grow to about 2.4m (8ft) high.

Clematis armandii

Evergreen tendril climber. This grows strongly, will reach 6m (20ft) and has clusters of small white flowers in April. The leaves are long, shining green and handsome. A specially good form is 'Snowdrift'. The plant is just a little tender and a south- or south-west-facing wall suits it well.

Clematis 'Comtesse de Bouchaud'

Deciduous, tendril climber. Large, soft pink flowers from June to August. Moderately vigorous growth.

Clematis 'Ernest Markham'

Deciduous, tendril climber. Large, petunia-purple flowers from June to September. Moderately vigorous.

Clematis 'Hagley Hybrid'

Deciduous, tendril climber. Large, light pink flowers from June to September. Moderately vigorous.

Clematis 'Lasurstern'

Clematis 'Huldine'

Deciduous, tendril climber. Large white flowers, mauve on the underside, from July to October. Moderately vigorous.

Clematis flammula

Deciduous, tendril climber. Abundant small, white, scented flowers in huge clusters from August to October. Vigorous. Will reach 3.5m (12ft) or more.

Clematis jackmanii

Deciduous, tendril climber. Abundant, medium size, violet-purple flowers from July to October. A variety named 'Superba' has larger iris-purple flowers.

Clematis 'Lasurstern'

Deciduous, tendril climber. Very large lavender-blue flowers in May and June and some smaller flowers later. Moderately vigorous.

Clematis macropetala
Deciduous, tendril climber. A little like *C. alpina* but the flowers are filled with small, petal-like segments making them resemble a ballerina's tutu. Typically the flowers are light violet-blue but 'Markham's Pink' has light rose flowers. All will reach 2.4m (8ft).

Clematis 'Marie Boisselot'
Deciduous, tendril climber. Large, broad-petalled white flowers appear from May to October. A moderately vigorous variety.

Clematis montana
Deciduous, tendril climber. Very vigorous with abundant small white or soft pink flowers which in some forms are scented. Can reach 9m (30ft). Colour and quality of bloom vary a lot so it is best to buy selected varieties such as 'Grandiflora', white and 'Rubens', pink.

Clematis 'Mrs Cholmondeley'
Deciduous, tendril climber. Very large, lavender-blue flowers from May to August. Moderately vigorous.

Clematis 'Ville de Lyon'

Clematis 'Perle D'Azur'

Clematis 'Nelly Moser'
Deciduous, tendril climber. Very large mauve flowers with carmine bars in May–June, with sometimes a few to follow later. Moderate vigour.

Clematis orientalis
Deciduous, tendril climber. Small, yellow, thick-petalled flowers in August followed by silvery seed heads. A very vigorous plant which will reach 6m (20ft).

Clematis 'Perle d'Azur'
Deciduous, tendril climber. Medium size, light blue flowers very freely produced from late June until late August. Fairly vigorous.

Clematis 'Royal Velours'
Deciduous, tendril climber. Small, deep reddish-purple flowers very freely produced in August and September. A vigorous plant.

Clematis tangutica
Deciduous, tendril climber. Small, yellow flowers in August–September, followed by silvery seed heads. Can reach 4m (13ft).

Clematis orientalis **with seed heads**

Clematis 'The President'
Deciduous, tendril climber. Very large purplish-blue flowers from June through to September. Moderate vigour.

Clematis 'Ville de Lyon'
Deciduous, tendril climber. Large carmine flowers from July to August. Moderate vigour.

Cotoneaster horizontalis
Deciduous shrub. Out in the open this shrub will spread out horizontally but if planted by a wall or fence it will fan out against it and give complete cover to a height of about 2.4m (8ft) without any support. The small leaves colour brilliantly before they fall in the autumn and the deep red berries are retained for a long time. The white flowers in June are much visited by honey bees.

Cytisus battandieri
Deciduous shrub. The long flexible stems of this 4m (13ft) Moroccan broom can be trained easily against a wall and it enjoys a warm sunny place. The leaves are covered in silky down and the erect clusters of yellow flowers that appear in May and in June are pineapple scented.

Euonymus fortunei radicans
Self-clinging evergreen. This very distinctive plant has rather small but very numerous leaves and stems which lie flat on the ground, rooting into it, but against a wall or fence will ascend, using the stem roots to cling like ivy. It can reach a height of 6m (20ft) and will thrive in sun or shade. A variety named 'Variegatus' has grey-green leaves edged with white – and often tinged pink.

Cytisus battandieri

Fremontodendron 'California Glory'

Euonymus fortunei 'Silver Queen'

Evergreen shrub. Unlike the last, this makes no stem roots and so cannot climb of its own accord but it can be trained to a height of about 2.4m (8ft). The leaves are quite large, shining green and heavily variegated with white. An invaluable shrub for enlivening the garden in the dark, winter months.

Wall-trained *Ficus carica*.

Fatshedera lizei

Evergreen sprawler. This hybrid between fatsia and ivy has large, deeply-lobed, evergreen leaves and long floppy stems which can be tied to any support to reach a height of about 2m (6ft). It will grow in sun or shade and is an excellent plant with which to give a sub-tropical effect to a patio or courtyard.

Ficus carica

Evergreen shrub. This is the common fig, a vigorous shrub frequently trained against walls where it is most likely to ripen its fruits. It is worth growing solely for its large, glossy, evergreen, deeply-lobed leaves, which are very handsome. It will grow in sun or shade but its fruits will only ripen in a warm, sunny place. It can reach 3m (10ft).

Forsythia suspensa

Deciduous shrub. This has the longest, most flexible stems of any forsythia and so is the best for training against walls. The flowers, which come in March–April, are light yellow and there is a variety, named 'Atrocaulis', with pale yellow flowers and purple stems which become almost black as they age.

Fremontodendron 'California Glory'

Evergreen shrub. The long stems of this free-flowering shrub can be trained to a height of about 6m (20ft). The leaves are slightly bronzy-green; the big, saucer-shaped flowers, from May to July, are bright yellow. This plant is not fully hardy but if trained against a south- or west-facing wall it will usually survive all but the most severe winters in milder parts of Britain. However, it is not naturally long lived and you may find that it has to be renewed from time to time.

Garrya elliptica

Evergreen shrub. This distinctive shrub has long grey-green catkins that develop in winter and remain for several months. There are male and female forms but the males give the best flower display. Garrya benefits from the protection of a south- or west-facing wall and is sufficiently sturdy to hold itself up but wires or trellis will be required on which to spread out the young stems.

Hedera canariensis 'Variegata'

Catkins of Garrya elliptica.

Hedera canariensis 'Variegata'

Self-clinging evergreen. A beautiful form of the Canary Island ivy, the leaves variegated with grey-green and cream. It is not as hardy as the British ivy but is excellent for sheltered patios and courtyards.

Hedera colchica 'Dentata Variegata'

Self-clinging evergreen. A large-leaved, fully hardy ivy with bold grey-green and creamy yellow variegation. It will thrive in either sun or shade.

Hedera helix 'Buttercup'

Self-clinging evergreen. A good all-yellow variety of the common ivy. It will grow in shade but leaf colour is best in good light and particularly on young leaves.

Hedera helix 'Goldheart'

Self-clinging evergreen. Another fine variety of the common ivy with a yellow blotch in the centre of each neat, dark green leaf. It colours best in good light.

Hedera helix 'Sagittifolia'

Self-clinging evergreen. Yet another variety of common ivy, distinguished by its rather small and narrow, five-lobed leaves.

Humulus lupulus 'Aureus'

Humulus lupulus 'Aureus'
A herbaceous twiner and the yellow-leaved form of the common hop, a hardy plant that dies down each autumn but is capable of making 4m (13ft) of growth the following spring and summer. Sunshine is required to produce the best leaf colour. Excellent for arbours, screens and so on where winter cover is not required.

Hydrangea petiolaris
Deciduous, self-clinging climber. The climbing hydrangea is very vigorous though rather slow starting and is capable eventually of reaching the top of a quite tall tree. It is also excellent on walls, whether sunny or shady. It clings by aerial roots like ivy and in June produces abundant flat clusters of white 'lace-cap' flowers.

Jasminum nudiflorum
Deciduous sprawler. This is the popular Winter Jasmine with yellow flowers from November until March. Left to its own devices it will sprawl but its stems can be readily tied to any support and against a wall it will reach 4m (13ft). Because the stems are green, the plant looks evergreen but in fact the little three-parted leaves fall in the autumn.

Jasminum officinale

Jasminum officinale
Deciduous twiner. This is the sweet scented jasmine which for centuries has been a popular plant for growing over arbours and summerhouses or training around a porch. The white flowers come successively from June to October. There is a variety named 'Argenteovariegata' with grey-green leaves edged with white.

Kerria japonica 'Pleniflora'
Deciduous shrub. This garden variety makes fewer but much longer stems than the single flowered kerria and also has fully double, orange-yellow flowers, for which reason it is often called Batchelor's Buttons. It is easily trained on a wall, fence or screen and makes an excellent display in May–June. It will thrive in sun or semi-shade.

Lathyrus latifolius

Herbaceous tendril climber. This strong growing plant, which can cover a considerable area in a single season, is known as the Everlasting Pea because it is a long lived perennial. Typically the flowers are rose-pink but there are lighter pink and white varieties. All can be increased by seed or by division in the spring.

Lonicera americana

Deciduous twiner. Despite its name, this fine honeysuckle has no connection with America. It is a natural hybrid between two European species and has fragrant yellow flowers flushed with reddish-purple in June–July. Vigorous.

Lonicera brownii

Semi-evergreen twiner. Another vigorous hybrid honeysuckle, often called the Scarlet Trumpet Honeysuckle because of the shape and colour of its flowers. They have no scent and come in May with more to follow in August.

Lonicera japonica

Evergreen twiner. Two forms of this are grown in gardens: 'Halliana', with green leaves and very fragrant

Lonicera × tellmanniana

white flowers which become light yellow with age and 'Aureoreticulata', with leaves heavily netted with yellow.

Lonicera periclymenum

Deciduous twiner. Fine native honeysuckle with spicily fragrant flowers. Two forms are grown, 'Early Dutch' or 'Belgica' and 'Late Dutch' or 'Serotina' but it is difficult to distinguish between them. Both have purplish-red and yellow flowers in June and 'Late Dutch' can be expected to produce more later in the summer.

Lonicera × tellmanniana

Deciduous twiner. A distinctive and vigorous hybrid honeysuckle with abundant, scentless, yellow flowers in June–July.

Lonicera tragophylla

Deciduous twiner. One of the parents of the last named with even larger, scentless, yellow flowers in June–July. It is even more resentful than most honeysuckles of hot, dry soil. Grows to 6m (20ft).

Lathyrus latifolius

Magnolia grandiflora

Evergreen tree. It may seem strange to include a tree among wall shrubs but in fact this handsome magnolia trains well and is frequently grown

Magnolia grandiflora

on sunny walls where there is 4 to 5m (13 to 16ft) of height available. It is valued primarily for its large, shining evergreen leaves but also for the great bowl-shaped white flowers in August–September which are more likely to be produced freely in a warm sunny place. 'Goliath' is a particularly good variety.

Parthenocissus henryana

Deciduous, self-clinging climber. This is one of those ornamental vines that gardeners are apt to lump together as Virginia Creepers. Its leaves, composed of several radiating leaflets, are dark green, pink and white. The plant is provided with adhesive pads which enable it to cling to anything. It is just a little tender but is ideal for a west-facing wall in a not too cold area.

Self-clinging *Parthenocissus henryana.*

Parthenocissus quinquefolia

Deciduous, tendril climber. This is the true Virginia Creeper, a very vigorous plant with large, five-lobed leaves which colour vividly in autumn. It cannot cling to walls but, with the aid of tendrils, will mount high into trees or go far over screens and pergolas.

Parthenocissus tricuspidata

Deciduous, self-clinging climber. The true popular name for this is Boston Ivy but it is often called Virginia Creeper or Ampelopsis. It is one of the most popular self-clinging wall plants, capable of covering whole buildings with its relatively small leaves which colour brilliantly in autumn. A particularly good form is 'Lowei'.

Passiflora caerulea

Deciduous, tendril climber. This is the Blue Passion Flower remarkable for the broad circle of blue-purple filaments in the otherwise white flower. There is an all-white variety named 'Constance Elliot'. Both are rather tender but may survive for many years on sunny walls in milder parts of Britain. Even when cut back by frost it can make 6m (20ft) of growth the following summer.

Passiflora caerulea sometimes produces yellow fruits.

Phygelius capensis

Evergreen shrub. In the open this plant will sprawl but against a wall it can be trained to a height of about 6m (20ft). The tubular flowers are scarlet and hang on curving stems in loose clusters from July to September. It is a little tender but usually survives against a sunny wall.

Polygonum baldschuanicum

Deciduous twiner. Popularly known as the Russian Vine, this is an extremely vigorous plant with huge clusters of small, creamy or pink-tinged flowers in September–October. Ideal for covering unsightly buildings or running high into trees.

Pyracantha atalantioides

Evergreen shrub. One of the strongest growing Firethorns, capable of clothing a high wall with little support. Its sprays of small, white flowers in early summer are followed by small but abundant scarlet fruits which usually remain for a long time.

Pyracantha 'Mohave'

Evergreen shrub. A moderately vigorous, hybrid Firethorn with quite large, orange berries.

Pyracantha rogersiana

Evergreen shrub. A relatively small-leaved species with fine sprays of white flowers in June followed by berries which are orange-red in variety 'Aurantiaca' and bright yellow in 'Flava'.

Pyracantha 'Orange Glow'

Evergreen shrub. Strong growing hybrid with spiny branches and quite large, orange-red berries.

Phygelius capensis

Polygonum baldschuanicum

Pyracantha rogersiana 'Flava'

Rosa 'Albertine', a *wichuraiana* rambler

Rosa 'Albéric Barbier'
Semi-evergreen rambler. This very vigorous rose has dark green, glossy leaves that, in a mild winter, will be almost completely retained. The double flowers are creamy-white and abundantly produced in June.

Rosa 'Albertine'
Deciduous rambler. Quite large, sweetly-scented, coppery-pink flowers in June. Strong, very thorny growth.

Rosa 'American Pillar'
Deciduous rambler, less lax than most. The very strong stems are quite stout and very thorny. Single, rose and white flowers are carried in large clusters in July.

Rosa 'Compassion'
Deciduous climber. Well shaped, apricot-pink flowers all summer. Moderate growth.

Rosa 'Danse du Feu'
Deciduous climber. Clusters of medium size, orange-red flowers all summer. Moderate growth.

Rosa 'Dublin Bay'
Deciduous climber. Clusters of medium size, crimson flowers all summer. Moderate growth.

Rosa 'Golden Showers'
Deciduous climber. Clusters of quite large, bright yellow flowers in June-July with a few more later in the summer. Moderate growth.

Rosa 'Pink Perpetue'

Rosa 'Handel'
Deciduous climber. Shapely, pink and white flowers of medium size, all summer. Grows to about 4m (13ft).

Rosa 'Kiftsgate'
Deciduous rambler. Huge clusters of single, creamy-white, richly-scented flowers in June–July. Once established, will reach 9m (30ft) and can ascend tall trees. Thorny.

Rosa 'Madame Alfred Carrière'
Deciduous climber. Small clusters of quite large, double flowers, cream in bud but white when fully open. They are sweetly scented and mainly produced in June–July but a few more usually come later. It has few thorns and is sufficiently vigorous to cover a house wall.

Rosa 'Madame Grégoire Staechelin'
Deciduous climber. Large, fully double, richly-scented flowers, carmine in bud, rose pink when open. Flowers in June–July only but there are large hips to follow, green becoming reddish-brown. Vigorous and fine for a house wall.

Rosa 'Maigold'
Deciduous climber. Medium size, semi-double, apricot-yellow flowers, mainly in June–July but a few to follow. Good, glossy green foliage. Moderately vigorous; very thorny.

Rosa 'Mermaid'
Deciduous climber. Large, single, light yellow flowers all summer. Glossy, dark green leaves and strong growth with big thorns but this rose is apt to die back if hard pruned. Only thin lightly and cut out dead or diseased stems. This variety does well trained on a partially shaded wall, if protected from hard frosts.

Rosa 'New Dawn'
Deciduous rambler. Clusters of medium size, double, pale pink flowers, borne throughout the summer months. Strong growth to 4m (13ft) or even more.

Rosa 'Maigold'

Rosa 'Pink Perpetue'

Deciduous climber. Clusters of medium size, rose-pink flowers all summer. Will reach 4m (13ft).

Rosa 'Schoolgirl'

Deciduous climber. Fairly large, apricot flowers all summer. Moderate vigour.

Rosa 'Seagull'

Deciduous rambler. Large clusters of small single, white flowers in June. Moderate vigour; will grow to about 4m (13ft).

Rosa 'Veilchenblau'

Deciduous rambler. Clusters of small, double, violet-purple flowers, fading to lilac in July. Will reach about 3.5m (12ft). Very few thorns.

Rosa 'Zéphirine Drouhin'

Deciduous climber. Large, fully double, rose-pink, scented flowers all summer. Thornless stems of moderate vigour to about 3m (10ft).

Rubus laciniatus

Deciduous bramble. This is popularly known as the Cut-leaved or Fern-leaved Blackberry, both of which give a good idea of its appearance. It grows just like an ordinary blackberry and produces good crops of well-flavoured berries but its leaves are finely divided and distinctly ornamental. It will reach 3m (10ft), has no natural means of support other than its thorns and, in gardens, must be tied to wires, posts or other supports.

Rubus phoenicolasius

Deciduous bramble. A relative of the blackberry, known as the Japanese Wineberry. The long stems are densely covered with purple bristles and the red fruits are much like loganberries but inferior in flavour. Stems need to be tied to supports.

Rubus phoenicolasius

45

Schizophragma integrifolium

Schizophragma integrifolium
Deciduous, self-clinging climber. This is a relative of the climbing hydrangea and climbs in the same way, by aerial roots. It differs in the formation of the flat flower clusters which have fewer but larger creamy-white bracts. The clusters can be as much as 30cm (1ft) in diameter and are very handsome in July–August. The plant can reach 9m (30ft).

Solanum crispum
Semi-evergreen sprawler. Left to its own devices this plant will make a big, sprawling bush or push its way up through stronger shrubs. It is more effective if trained against a sunny wall or screen or over a pergola where its large clusters of flowers will be well displayed. They are purplish-blue with a cone of yellow stamens in the centre like those of a potato to which it is related. Its popular name is Potato Vine. It flowers from June to September. 'Glasnevin' is a good, free-flowering variety.

Tropaeolum speciosum
Herbaceous twiner. This striking plant has rather fleshy roots and long, slender stems with small, deeply-lobed leaves and small but very numerous, scarlet, nasturtium-like flowers. It is popularly known as the Flame Flower and it likes to scramble up through other plants. In Scotland and the north of England where it grows particularly well, it can often be seen covering yew hedges with trails of brilliant scarlet flowers from July onwards. Plants should be obtained in pots, preferably in spring, and be planted without root breakage in fairly rich, rather moist soil.

Solanum crispum 'Glasnevin'

Trachelospermum jasminoides

Evergreen twiner. The glossy dark green leaves make good cover for a wall and the small but abundant white flowers in July–August fill the air with sweet jasmine perfume. There is a variety named 'Variegatum' with cream variegated leaves. Plants are a little tender but in most places safe on a south-facing wall.

Vitis 'Brant'

Deciduous, tendril climber. A handsome hybrid vine with leaves that become bronzy-red in the autumn except for the veins which remain green. The juice of the small, black fruits is pleasant to drink or can be used to make wine.

Vitis coignetiae

Deciduous, tendril climber. One of the most vigorous of all vines, capable of reaching the top of a tall tree. The leaves are also very large, up to 30cm (1ft) across and more or less round. They colour vividly in the autumn.

Vitis vinifera 'Purpurea'

Deciduous, tendril climber. A decorative variety of the common grape vine with claret-red leaves, turning to a spectacular deep purple.

Wisteria sinensis

Wisteria floribunda

Deciduous twiner. A species of moderate vigour, excellent for covering arbours, pergolas and so on. Typically the long, scented flower trails in May-June are violet-blue but there are white, pink and purple varieties.

Wisteria sinensis

Deciduous twiner. This is the strongest growing kind, capable of ascending to the tops of tall trees. It is often propagated by seeds but seedlings tend to be variable in quality so it is wise to buy either from a reliable nurseryman or while the plants are in flower. Colour can be anything from a rather pale greyish-blue to clear lilac-blue and there is a white variety named 'Alba'. There are also numerous garden varieties, mainly of Japanese origin, which are probably hybrids with W. *floribunda* and have variously coloured flowers: white, light blue, dark blue and pink.

Vitis vinifera 'Brant'

INDEX AND ACKNOWLEDGEMENTS

Picture credits

Pat Brindley: 11(b),13(b),14(l),15(t,b),16(r),17(b),22(t),32(t),
 34(t,b),35(t),36(t),37(r),38(r),39(t,b),42(br),43,44(t,b),46(b).
Lyn and Derek Gould: 17(t).
Arthur Hellyer: 12,16(l),46(t).
ICI: 27(bl, br).
Harry Smith Horticultural Photographic Collection: 4/5,6,7(t,b),
 9,10,11(t),13(t),14(r),18,20,23(t,b),24,25(t),26,28/9,30,31(t,b),
 32(b),33(l,r),35(b),36(b),37(l),38(l),40(t,b),41,42(t,bl),45,47(t,b).
Michael Warren: 1,22(b),27(t).

Artwork by Simon Roulstone